Spirit

RIT Archives Chapbook Series

Series Editor: Elizabeth Call

The RIT Archives Chapbook Series uncovers the lesser-known stories that have shaped Rochester Institute of Technology's history and culture. Written and researched by students in partnership with the RIT Archives, each volume highlights moments of innovation, resilience, and creativity that might otherwise remain hidden. Compact and accessible, these chapbooks bring archival research into the hands of the wider community, connecting past and present in ways that inspire reflection and spark new ideas.

As RIT approaches its two hundredth anniversary, the series affirms the importance of storytelling as a form of stewardship, celebrating the diverse voices and experiences that have defined the university while equipping the next generation of scholars with the tools to carry those stories forward.

SPIRIT

Autumn Bernava

Edited by Elizabeth Call

RIT Press
Rochester, New York

Published and distributed by:
RIT Press
90 Lomb Memorial Drive
Rochester, New York 14623
https://press.rit.edu

Printed in the United States of America

ISBN 978-1-956313-45-1 (print)
ISBN 978-1-956313-46-8 (electronic)

We gather on the traditional territory of the Onöndowa'ga:' or "the
people of the Great Hill." In English, they are known as Seneca people,
"the keeper of the western door." They are one of the six nations that
make up the sovereign Haudenosaunee Confederacy.

   We honor the land on which RIT was built and recognize the unique
relationship that the Indigenous stewards have with this land. That
relationship is the core of their traditions, cultures, and histories. We
recognize the history of genocide, colonization, and assimilation of
Indigenous people that took place on this land. Mindful of these
histories, we work towards understanding, acknowledging, and
ultimately reconciliation.

Front cover: Spirit the tiger visits the library with an unknown student,
1963. Back cover: The RIT Tiger Committee greets Spirit the cub at the
Rochester airport, 1963.
Designed by Marnie Soom

Contents

BEVIER BUILDING, SCHOOL OF APPLIED ARTS

EASTMAN BUILDING, SCHOOL OF INDUSTRIAL AND HOUSEHOLD ARTS

GEORGE H. CLARK BUILDING

Rochester Institute of Technology
AT ROCHESTER, NEW YORK
on the
New York Central

Images of Rochester Athenaeum and Mechanics Institute downtown campus, featuring pictures of students in classes from the early 1900s. *Rochester Athenaeum and Mechanics Institute records, RITArc.0704, RIT Archives.*

Rochester Institue of Technology pamphlet, ca. 1960. *Rochester Athenaeum and Mechanics Institute records, RITArc.0704, RIT Archives.*

Universities have existed in the United States since the early colonial period, but it wasn't until the 1800s that American university culture began to blossom into the form we recognize today.[1] Brotherhoods evolved into fraternities, athletic teams became central to campus life, and complex intercommunity dynamics began to reflect the broader American melting pot. Spurred in part by the height of the Industrial Revolution, the country experienced a dramatic shift in the demand for secondary education. The traditional pathway of high school graduates moving directly into the workforce was no longer sufficient, as workers now needed to receive deeper training in order to operate increasingly complex machinery. Men—and women—began seeking both education and connection to expand not only their knowledge but also their personal growth.

In response to these changing conditions, cities established schools to meet these new demands. Social clubs and libraries began offering night courses, and older institutions that had originally focused on the liberal arts started incorporating courses in the science and mechanical fields. American society was no longer primarily rural and agrarian but instead was rapidly shifting toward mechanized agriculture and large-scale factory production to support a growing population. This transformation created an urgent need for cities to provide an education that aligned with the evolving requirements of industry and culture.

In Rochester, the Franklin Institute began offering night classes in response to increased industrialization along the Erie Canal routes. Founded in 1826, and initially catering to boys seeking to enter the workforce with a higher level of education to increase their earning potential, the Franklin Institute marked the earliest beginnings of what would become the Rochester Institute

of Technology (RIT).[2] It was absorbed by the Rochester Athenaeum in 1829, the year recognized in RIT's institutional history as its founding date.

The goal of the institute was to offer instruction to anyone wishing to expand their knowledge of science and technology. In part, it also served the Masonic Order of Rochester, a dominant guild in the city that sought to employ boys with higher education levels to reduce the need for traditional apprenticeships.[3]

This interaction with the community was essential to the institute's early days. Founded just fifteen years after the city itself and only three years after the Erie Canal reached Rochester, the school's history became closely intertwined with Rochester's. While growing, the Rochester Athenaeum also merged with other Rochesterian societies, including the Rochester Literary Company, the Young Men's Society, and the Mechanics Literary Association. At times, due to financial weaknesses, the young institute struggled to remain afloat, and it moved locations several times for economic reasons. Without a permanent home, the Rochester Athenaeum found itself facing continuous issues such as rent, stability, and what to do with its material possessions. Due to the lack of physical security and its monetary needs, the Rochester Athenaeum began selling its library collection. It wasn't until 1885 when over fifty Rochester industries—including Bausch and Lomb—began once again pushing for further education of employees that the Athenaeum became financially secure.[4]

The Morrill Act of 1862 contributed to a better financial future for the institute's economic woes. The goal of this act was to establish public colleges across the United States through the sale of federal land.[5] Specializing in the creation of schools for mechanics and agriculture, the Morrill Act was meant to increase the accessibility of

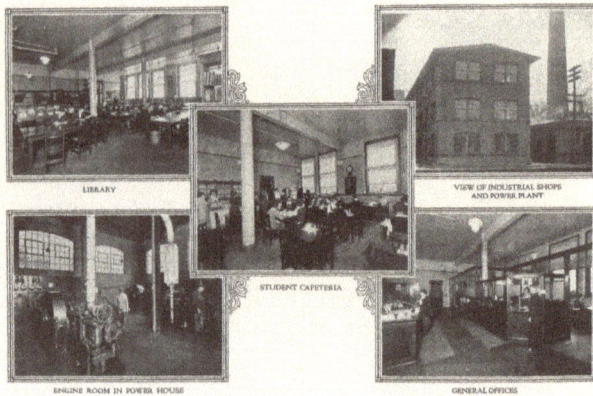

Images of Rochester Athenaeum and Mechanics Institute downtown campus, featuring pictures of students in classes from the early 1900s. *Rochester Athenaeum and Mechanics Institute records, RITArc.0704, Box 4, Folder 4, RIT Archives.*

Images of Rochester Athenaeum and Mechanics Institute downtown campus, featuring pictures of housing and classrooms from the early 1900s. *Rochester Athenaeum and Mechanics Institute records, RITArc.0704, Box 4, Folder 4, RIT Archives.*

these courses. At the time, the majority of the students partaking in mechanics and in classes offered at agrarian and mercantile institutes were white men. Women were beginning to apply more often as home economics courses also arose, but there were also separate colleges being endowed for minority groups.[6] The Rochester Athenaeum—an accumulation of schools with this very goal—applied for the land grant, hoping to find a permanent place for the campus. Unfortunately, it was not able to secure the funds, although a sizable amount was allocated toward the creation of Cornell University, just two hours south of Rochester.

This era was followed by schools trying to find their unique focuses—their spirit. While older institutions such as Harvard pushed for liberal arts to remain just as relevant as mechanics and engineering, technical education became equally valued as trade unions recognized this need more widely across the country. The

Rochester Athenaeum's old connections with the Masons and other Rochesterian guilds remained relevant as it continued to produce the kinds of workers those groups desired. In 1891, the Rochester Athenaeum took the next step in its history, merging with the recently established Mechanics Institute to become the Rochester Athenaeum and Mechanics Institute (RAMI). At this time, a true emergence of student character began to arise as well, as students became more involved in university life instead of simply attending for education alone.

This ripple of change echoed throughout the country as large universities, already stratified in part by socioeconomic status, grew even more divided. Fraternities emerged across American campuses, creating a formalized hierarchy that signaled a young man's social standing within the institution.[8] Alongside Greek life, the rise of collegiate athletic teams expanded opportunities for student involvement and fostered a growing spectator culture.

COURSES

TEACHER TRAINING
Industrial
Home Economics
Art

HOME ECONOMICS
Lunch Room Management
Dietetics
Costume Design and
Trade Dressmaking
Home Making
Trade Millinery

APPLIED & FINE ARTS
Costume Design
Architecture
Design and
Interior Decoration
Illustration and
Advertising Art
Occupational Therapy

INDUSTRIAL COURSES
Mechanical
Electrical
Chemical
Electrical Construction
Mechanical Drawing
Auto Ignition

TRADE COURSES
Machine Shop Practice
Lithography

Further information concerning any of the Courses will be furnished on application to the Registrar of Rochester Athenaeum and Mechanics Institute, at Rochester, New York.

A course list of the Rochester Athenaeum and Mechanics Institute classes before their rebranding to RIT, from an Athenaeum booklet published in the early 1900s. *Rochester Athenaeum and Mechanics Institute records, RITArc.0704, Box 4, Folder 4, RIT Archives.*

These developments added another layer of social stratification, particularly for those who played on the teams. As the world of college sports and performative masculinity grew, so did the level of competition, with many students using athletics as a means to elevate their social position.[9]

It became a mark of pride to be among those selected to participate in these coveted circles, which helped define a shifting campus life increasingly shaped by student culture. Sports and fraternities offered participants a pathway to social relevance, especially within colleges where economic background played a significant role in determining one's place in the campus hierarchy.

At RAMI, however, student life initially centered almost exclusively on academics. Determined to make the most of their studies, men enrolled to learn drawing and mechanics, while women focused on domestic sciences. In these early years, before programs and extracurricular opportunities expanded, students attended RAMI primarily for educational instruction rather than community-building or social activities.

It was not until the early 1900s, particularly in the years leading up to World War I, that RAMI began developing a school culture that echoed the traditions emerging at larger institutions across the country. A key milestone came in 1912 with the publication of the school's first yearbook, *The M.I. Book, Volume 1*, later known as the *Ramikin*. The opening page declared a sense of identity and belonging that would resonate with students for generations: "This Book is the first record of our growing school spirit, born of a well beloved Faculty, congenial work and good comradeship. From the moment you have one in your possession, may you call it with pride & satisfaction not M. I. Book, but, My Book."[10] This statement marked a pivotal shift, signaling the emergence of a shared school spirit and a developing student culture that extended beyond the classroom.

A page from the RIT *PSIMAR*, featuring a graphic of the RIT wrestlers in their singlets. PSIMAR *collection, RITArc.0803, RIT Archives.*

This moment may have marked the beginning of campus culture at RIT as we recognize it today. The year 1912 also saw the introduction of organized, school-sponsored athletics and the emergence of fraternities and sororities. *The M.I. Book* includes team photographs of the inaugural basketball, baseball, and track teams, along with images of the first two fraternities and the first sorority. It also highlights a range of clubs open to both men and women, including but not limited to a drama club and an art league.

Despite its strong display of emerging school pride and spirit, the first volume of the *Ramikin* was remembered as "a literary success, but a complete financial disaster."[11] As the nation approached wartime, RAMI needed new ways to support its developing student culture. In 1916, the school hosted a Halloween party to raise funds for the continued production of the yearbook. With the onset of World War I, RAMI shifted further, launching intensive six-week training programs to prepare soldiers for deployment. During this period, previously gender-segregated programs began opening to both men and women, reflecting broader social changes.[12] Despite these shifts, the institute maintained strong connections with Rochester's unions, remaining grounded in its working-class origins even as it adapted to global uncertainty.

In terms of gender inclusivity, RAMI was notably more open to women than many other institutions of its time were. From the institute's early years, women were allowed to enroll in various art courses. In 1916, total enrollment at RAMI reached 7,592 students. Of these, 4,974 were enrolled in the Department of Household Arts and Sciences, a predominantly female division, meaning that women comprised more than half of the student body.[13] This stood in stark contrast to many universities across the country, where women were often treated as outsiders.[14]

The RAMI Delta Omicron class of 1928–1929. Hunt, fourth from right, first row; Schutt, end of first row. *Ramikin* yearbook, 127. *RIT Archives.*

The question of women's place in higher education has been debated repeatedly throughout history. Even today, conversations persist about whether women, especially women of color, belong in certain fields, particularly those related to science, technology, engineering, and mathematics (STEM). Women in these areas often face higher dropout rates than their male counterparts do.[15] At a historically technological institution like RAMI, this raises an important question: How have women been affected by such divisions and doubts?

The answer is more encouraging than one might expect. Women have long been central to shaping school spirit and student culture at the institute. From the beginning, women had access to courses, particularly in domestic sciences, and were supported by faculty who advocated for their rights to learn and to be compensated fairly. As the school began to cultivate a more vibrant student life, women emerged as key leaders, particularly in student publications.

Two prominent examples are Miss Elizabeth Hunt, the editor in chief of RAMI's first student newspaper (established in 1928), and Miss Thelma Schute, the editor in chief of the 1929 *Ramikin*, the institute's yearbook. Both women were also members of Delta Omicron, one of RAMI's earliest sororities, whichh was founded to foster friendship, growth, and mutual support among women.[16] Their leadership solidified the place of women not only within academic life but also at the heart of student identity and expression.

These women-led publications played a crucial role in the evolution of student culture. The *PSIMAR* in particular was among the first platforms to publicly showcase student spirit, opinions, and creative thought. Both a voice and a historical record, it captured student passions that

PSIMAR, Vol. 1, No. 1, published October 12, 1928. PSIMAR *collection, RITArc.0803, RIT Archives.*

Sixth edition of the PSIMAR paper, edited by Elizabeth Hunt and featuring a special on Thelma Schutt, published May 9, 1929. *PSIMAR collection, RITArc.0803, RIT Archives.*

would echo through later RIT publications. At its founding in 1928, the paper declared its mission: "By providing a means of expression for student opinion, it has served to clear up many a misunderstanding and prejudice; it is to be hoped that this good work will be continued."[17] In articulating pride, unity, and identity, women editors helped define and preserve the spirit of the student body— ensuring that women were not mere observers of campus culture but rather creators of it.

The second edition of the *PSIMAR*, published on November 16, 1928, featured several letters to the editor that reflected student perspectives on campus life and attitudes toward the institute. One such letter from W. N. Fenninger read: "I am sure the 'Psimar' will help to improve the school spirit. I hope many more will contribute to it and use the paper as a forum for the expression of ideas on student activities as well as the reporting of news, including humorous news."[18] Fenninger's hope proved prophetic, as student publications would become a cornerstone of the institute's evolving culture.

Moving out of the early 1900s and into midcentury, the institute underwent a series of significant transformations. In 1945, the *Ramikin* was renamed the *Techmila*, reflecting the institution's official transition to Rochester Institute of Technology (RIT), a name selected by the postwar planning committee. Just a year earlier, in 1944, the *PSIMAR* ceased publication, partially due to declining enrollment during World War II; only seventeen men remained in the senior class.[19] The student newspaper would not return until 1951, when it was revived under a new name, the *Reporter*. This relaunch marked the beginning of a new era for the institute. As the school entered the postwar period, its identity solidified and the foundations of student spirit and culture were firmly laid.

Above: Crosses dot the open grounds of the Henrietta campus during a Vietnam War protest, 1969. *RIT University News slide collection, RITArc.0464, Box 47, Image 21, RIT Archives.*

Right: Students protest the Vietnam War in the Student Union on the new Henrietta campus, 1969. *RIT University News slide collection, RITArc.0464, Box 47, Image 24, RIT Archives.*

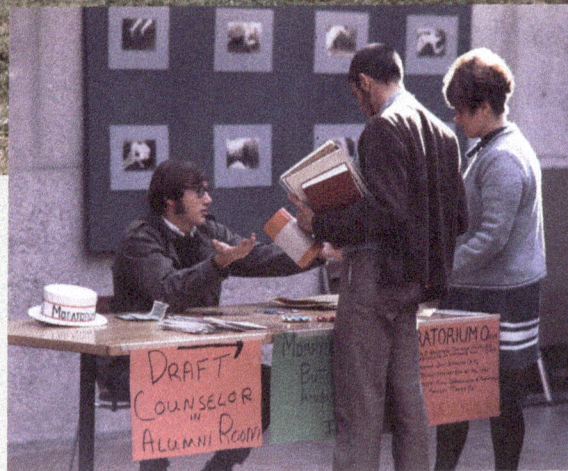

In the mid-twentieth century, colleges across the United States experienced a sharp decline in enrollment during World War II, followed by a dramatic surge in the postwar years. By the 1950s and 1960s, institutions were suddenly flooded with new students, expanded academic programs, and returning veterans seeking education through opportunities such as the GI Bill. As the nation transitioned from active warfare to the tensions of the Cold War, interest in science and technology surged. Unlike the earlier focus on mechanical skills and wartime industry, this new era was driven by the power of applied science, particularly in the race to reach the moon.

Chemistry and physics textbooks were rewritten, and classroom methods shifted toward hands-on, experimental learning, all in pursuit of restoring American educational superiority.[20] Meanwhile, since the educational boom of the 1920s following World War I, improvements in secondary education had made high school diplomas increasingly accessible. The belief that an educated citizenry could better serve the nation in times of conflict led to expanded access to K–12 schooling, which in turn fueled the rapid growth of universities and graduate programs.

To sustain this surge in educational demand, the federal government significantly increased its investment in higher education. Prior to the 1900s, federal support had largely taken the form of land grants, such as those provided under the Morrill Act. However, the economic expansion fueled by wartime production enabled the government to allocate far greater financial resources to emerging universities. In the years leading up to World War II, national college enrollment neared 1.5 million students, and those numbers rose dramatically after the war as veterans entered or returned to higher education.[21]

In 1944, Congress passed the Servicemen's Readjustment Act, better known as the GI Bill, which provided financial support for veterans' education and housing. Within just twelve years, the bill redistributed more than $14 billion in educational aid and approximately $33 billion in home ownership assistance.[22] The program continued during the Korean War and Vietnam War eras, offering veterans up to thirty-six months of tuition coverage after a standard two-year enlistment—sufficient to complete a bachelor's degree. Nearly ten million veterans took advantage of this opportunity.[23]

However, the GI Bill's promise of access to education and housing was not equally realized by all veterans. While the legislation was being developed, southern lawmakers intentionally structured it to disproportionately benefit white veterans. Because eligibility required an honorable discharge, many Black veterans, who were dishonorably discharged at higher rates due to discriminatory practices, were effectively excluded from its benefits.[24] As a result, many Black veterans were forced into low-paying, menial work. Even those who qualified faced additional barriers, including segregated schools, discriminatory teachers who denied them necessary training, and restricted access to universities. This was especially true in the South, where many institutions refused to admit Black students, and in the North, where admission often came slowly and grudgingly.

Amid this uneven landscape of educational access, federal support for science and technology surged. The National Science Foundation (NSF), proposed during World War II but formally established in 1950, grew rapidly in importance after the Soviet launch of Sputnik in 1957. Between 1958 and 1959, its federal budget increased dramatically from $40 million to $134 million.[25] These funds were directed to research institutions to accelerate advancements in technological and biological sciences and to cultivate an educated workforce that could help the

United States compete in the Cold War. This expansion was further supported by defense-related funding and new federal legislation aimed at strengthening education nationwide.

Two major acts exemplified this shift: the National Defense Education Act (NDEA) of 1957 and, five years later, the Higher Education Act of 1963. The NDEA, in particular, encouraged study in science, foreign languages, and mathematics, while also providing broader financial support through lower-interest student loans and expanded university funding. Like the GI Bill, both acts increased access to higher education and stimulated dramatic enrollment growth; between 1960 and 1970, class sizes nearly doubled from 3.6 million to 7.5 million students.[26] These measures reflected a new era of substantial federal involvement in education, driven by the urgency of global competition and the strategic value of an educated populace.

This influx of federal support came with clear priorities, and most funding was channeled into the sciences. During this period, science and technical education were heralded as the solution to nearly all national ambitions, and RIT positioned itself accordingly as a center for higher education in technology. [27] The 1950s marked a turning point as RIT introduced its first baccalaureate programs, transitioning from a mechanical institute into a fully recognized university. This decade also saw a rise in student enrollment, the launch of graduate programs, and a broadening of academic offerings. RIT's growth reflected national trends; by the 1965–1966 academic year, enrollment had reached 3,181 students, the largest in its history to that point.[28]

Amid local and national development, RIT began planning a major relocation. Originally situated in downtown Rochester and woven into the fabric of the city, the institute faced pressures as suburban expansion and postwar urban restructuring transformed the landscape. The construction of the New York State Thruway and the "Inner Loop" threatened existing campus structures, including the Eastman Building. In 1961, under the leadership of President Mark Ellingson, the Board of Trustees voted to purchase 1,300 acres of farmland in Henrietta, land that was expected to serve the university "for the next hundred years."[29] This decision initiated a decade of profound transformation, with the move to Henrietta and rapidly increasing enrollment laying the foundation for the RIT we know today.

Rochester was not immune to the sweeping social and political shifts of the 1960s. The highway project slated to cut through RIT's downtown campus was initially promoted as a symbol of postwar urban progress, intended to accommodate the city's growing population. Planned by the New York State Department of Public Works, the project would have physically divided the original campus in two. Though touted as architecturally modern, the highway's placement reflected the troubling social realities of the era: it cut directly through areas labeled "slums," including the predominantly African American Third Ward. Marketed as the "Urban Design Project," this wave of redevelopment would later be criticized as "Segregation by Design."[30] Similar inner-loop highways targeting low-income neighborhoods were implemented in cities across the nation—RIT simply found itself situated in the midst of these broader patterns.

By 1964, the same year the campus relocation was announced, RIT students were becoming increasingly engaged with civil rights activism occurring nationwide and were also beginning to confront injustices in their own community. In a letter to the *Reporter* magazine, student Eric T. Hepborn highlighted racial inequities in Rochester's housing market: "In the very city of Rochester, Negroes with PhDs and other learned sepia professionals find it very difficult to obtain satisfactory housing. Out of the available real estate in Rochester, people of color have access to exactly 10 per cent. Most of this 'available' property is located in some abominable region unfit for a menial, let alone a professional."[31] Hepborn concluded pointedly: "Great article, Mr. Fredericks, but truth compels me to conclude that the South has no patent on this disease [of racism]."[31]

Although RIT was not the site of frequent physical demonstrations like nearby University of Rochester was, students actively participated in the national movement. Some traveled to marches in Washington, DC; others raised funds to support civil rights initiatives in the South; and many used student publications such as newspapers and yearbooks to voice their opinions.[32]

As classes began to split between the downtown campus and the developing Henrietta location, both the school and the nation found themselves in a state of upheaval. Greg Evans, the student body president and a member of the class of 1969, recalled the climate of the era: "The Vietnam War loomed over everything. We weren't holding demonstrations like the University of Rochester, but several of us went to Washington, D.C., and we discussed the news every single night."[33]

While RIT's campus culture remained relatively peaceful, the threat of war and social unrest weighed heavily on students. The 1964 edition of the *Techmila* opened with a foreword reflecting this global anxiety: "The changes at RIT are part of an awesome restlessness that is stirring in every part of the globe. We are no longer citizens of just a country because this revolution is making us citizens of the world, and our curricula must prepare us for the challenge."[34] This statement articulated a student awareness of global responsibility, emphasizing the role of education in preparing individuals to defend human rights and navigate a rapidly changing world. As both a platform for student expression and a record of campus life, the *Techmila* captured the rhythm of student experiences and their broader social consciousness.

Only about a month after the 1964 yearbook was

Left: Students hold protest signs in the Student Union during the Vietnam War, 1969. *RIT University News slide collection, RITArc.0464, Box 47, Image 26, RIT Archives.*
Right: Students display a papier-mâché cross in the Student Union as commentary on the Vietnam War, 1969. *RIT University News slide collection, RITArc.0464, Box 47, Image 23, RIT Archives.*

released, tensions in Rochester reached a breaking point. Students, who were already transitioning from the downtown campus to the new Henrietta location, found themselves in the midst of civil unrest. The Third Ward, still home to parts of the university's downtown facilities, became a focal point as the proposed Inner Loop highway threatened to displace residents. Frustration over racial discrimination and overcrowded living conditions erupted into three days of riots. The National Guard was called in and nearly 1,000 people were arrested, and while the iconic campus buildings avoided damage, the unrest left a lasting impact on the student body.

Above: Images of a Vietnam War protest hosted by the RIT students in 1969; signs reading "use your power" urge students to advocate against the draft. *RIT University Photography collection, RITArc.0672, folder 42-70c, RIT Archives.*

Above right: Images of a Vietnam War protest hosted by the RIT students in 1969, featuring the masses gathered on the Henrietta campus. *RIT University Photography collection, RITArc.0672, folder 42-70b, RIT Archives.*

Right: A student speaker addresses gathered students on the Henrietta campus during a Vietnam War protest in 1969. *RIT University Photography collection, RITArc.0672, folder 50-I-70, RIT Archives.*

Far right: Speakers talk to gathered students during a Vietnam War protest in 1969 on the Henrietta campus. *RIT University Photography collection, RITArc.0672, folder 50-I-70, RIT Archives.*

Below right: Student speakers address gathered students on the Henrietta campus during a Vietnam War protest in 1969. *RIT University Photography collection, RITArc.0672, folder 50-I-70, RIT Archives.*

Left: A window-view photograph shows gathered students on RIT's Henrietta campus hills during a Vietnam War protest rally in 1969. *RIT University Photography collection, RITArc.0672, folder 42-70a, RIT Archives.*

Below left: A young girl sits on the shoulders of an attendee at a Vietnam War protest rally on the RIT Henrietta campus in 1969. *RIT University Photography collection, RITArc.0672, folder 42-70d, RIT Archives.*

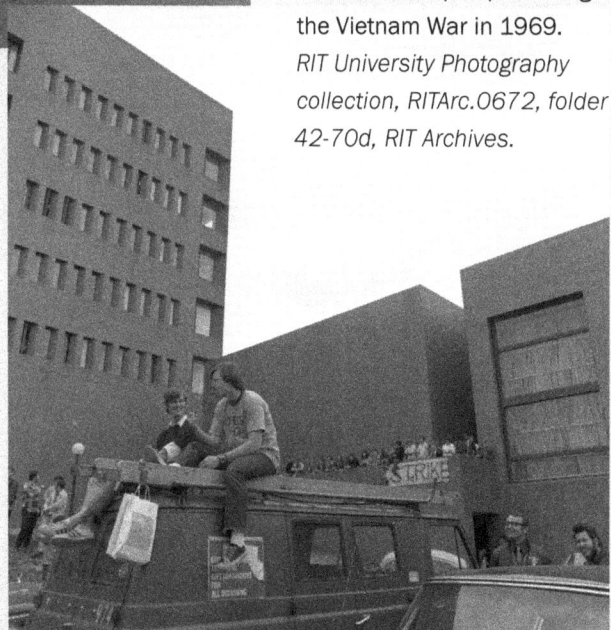

Below right: Students sit on a van parked near a gathered rally of RIT students on the Henrietta campus protesting the Vietnam War in 1969. *RIT University Photography collection, RITArc.0672, folder 42-70d, RIT Archives.*

Despite the strong presence of activism in many student publications of the time, not all students shared the same perspectives. For every impassioned letter to the editor or anti-war protest, there were pro-war rallies and students who supported US involvement abroad. Others formed a "silent majority," neither aligning with activist sentiment nor engaging in direct opposition. For many, daily life continued with a sense of normalcy: athletes trained and competed, fraternities and sororities hosted formals and socials, and students embraced moments of leisure amid uncertainty.

In the post–World War II era, RIT athletics began to gain momentum and community attention, particularly after standout seasons. After the university adopted the name Rochester Institute of Technology, athletic teams were informally known as the "Techmen," with the wrestling team often referred to as the "Matmen." However, during the 1955–1956 basketball season, when the team went undefeated, RIT *Reporter* staff member Harry Watts suggested adopting a more formidable collegiate mascot.[35] It was during that season that Watts began referring to RIT athletes as the "Tigers," a name that quickly resonated with students. Variations of the nickname spread rapidly across publications, inspiring monikers such as the "Tigerettes" for the women's fencing team and the "Tiger Sharks" for the swim team. Even the cheer squad incorporated the branding into their chants. By 1956, the tiger emblem appeared prominently in the yearbook, solidifying the mascot's place in campus identity.

A 1957 April Fools edition of the *Reporter* jokingly proposed sending a committee to Africa to acquire a live mascot. The satirical article read: "A recommendation was then made with regard to school spirit. It was the feeling of the committee that the soaring school spirit should be reinforced by the addition of a live mascot to the athletic department. This, the committee proposed, could be done inexpensively by sending a council member on a safari

Printed article advertising an alumni basketball game, one of the earliest references to RIT's "Tigers," 1962. *Collection on Spirit (Tiger), RITArc.0035, Box 1, RIT Archives.*

to Africa to capture two baby tigers."[36] While humorous at the time, the idea of a live tiger mascot captured student imagination and lingered on campus for years.

By 1963, during the transition from the downtown campus to the new Henrietta location, members of the Alpha Pi Omega fraternity put forward a serious proposal to obtain a Bengal tiger cub—not through poaching, but through fundraising and purchase. David Page (class of 1966) led the newly formed Tiger Committee, which developed a plan to bring the cub to RIT. The committee raised $1,000 by selling $1 stock shares that granted students symbolic "ownership" of what would become the school's first live mascot.

We display our natural bend
In the sports where we contend.
And the fame accumulated
Is, like energy, soon dissipated.

151

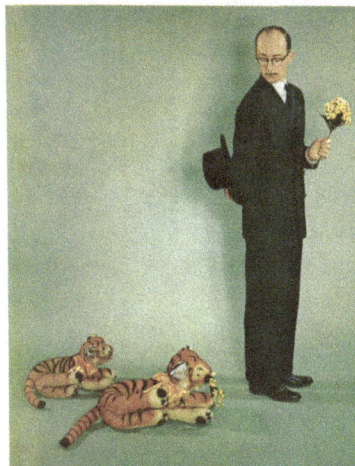

We throw a sweet bouquet
Of memories from 90's gay,
To those of you who did attend
The doings of our Spring Weekend

163

The 1956 edition of the *Techmila* features some of the first tiger imagery; in this case, two stuffed tigers reposed throughout the book as section dividers. *1956* Techmila, *p. 151, RIT Archives.*

Although the tiger was considered a campus symbol, it was housed and cared for at the Seneca Park Zoo. Members of the Tiger Committee, after receiving training, were allowed to bring the cub to campus events. A student poll officially named the tiger "Spirit," an acronym for "Student Pride at RIT," cementing the mascot as a living emblem of campus identity.

Spirit's appearances, however, were short-lived. Within four months, he had grown too large to be safely brought to campus. Despite this, students continued to celebrate him, organizing events such as a "Tiger Birthday Party" held on July 29, 1964, at the Seneca Park Zoo to mark the mascot's first year.

Page helped carry the tiger mascot tradition forward by becoming one of the first people to wear a tiger costume at RIT events. His leadership in acquiring Spirit cemented the tiger as the university's official symbol for generations to come. Spirit's influence was immediately visible: the mascot appeared in that year's *Techmila*, featured in photographs alongside athletic teams and students as well as in the yearbook's visual design and branding.

Spirit's arrival marked the beginning of a new era, one in which RIT fully embraced its identity as a university rather than a trade-focused institute. By aligning with the broader collegiate culture of the 1960s, RIT stepped into a transformative period of campus life. While earlier students had attended the school before degrees were offered and before the move to the Henrietta campus, this new generation entered with a shared symbol, a growing sense of identity, and a unifying campus spirit around which to build a modern university culture.

HELP PUT A TIGER ON OUR TEAM BUY A SHARE OF TIGER STOCK $1.00

RIT's Flying Tiger Arrives!

Name Tiger Contest Set

The latest addition to the campus, the RIT Tiger, is currently nameless.

The three month old Bengalese mascot, which resides in Seneca Park Zoo, desperately needs a name. Officers of the RIT Tiger Committee (also the newest organization on campus) have announced the start of a school-wide contest to find a suitable name for the tiger cub.

Anyone — students, staff, or faculty — is invited to submit their entry to the Student Activities Center anytime from now until noon on Wednesday Nov. 27. The Student Activities Center is located on Clarissa St. near the Library.

An award of a set of tickets for one couple for Spring Weekend will be given to the person who submits the name thought most suitable by the judges, and in case of a duplicate entry, the one submitted earliest will be winner.

Furry Feline Cub Captures Hearts of Awaiting Crowd

It was a cold, windy Wednesday night at nearly one in the morning, but despite the time and the weather a crowd was present at the airport to greet the baby Bengal. Dave Page, RIT's "mascot," expressed what seemed to be the general feeling by greeting his 20 lb., golden, black and white striped replacement with a broad grin.

More than 50 members of the student body, faculty, and administration were on hand to greet RIT's tiger when he arrived at the airport on an American Airlines plane at 12:45 a.m. on Oct. 29.

Mr. and Mrs. A. Stephen Walls, Miss Deanne Molinari, and Dr. James R. Campbell, among others, were in attendance when the motorcade left the Student Activities Center shortly before midnight on its way to the airport.

The plane was twice delayed and arrived approximately 15 minutes later than originally planned, but the RIT'ers were

there to greet it, with cheers and "welcome homes" even going out onto the runway to meet the plane.

Several members of the WITR staff were on hand to record and transmit proceedings, and the campus radio station remained on the air two hours longer than usual to announce the Tiger's arrival.

Dave Page, until the purchase of the baby Bengal, RIT's "mascot," was the first student to see the cat, and his first informative comment, "He's got big, brown eyes."

TIGER MEETS TIGER—Dave Page, RIT's human stand-in, proudly holds aloft the flesh-and-blood version of the real thing, which arrived at the Rochester airport last Wednesday morning. (Photo by Frank Feldman)

STOCK CERTIFICATE

This is to Certify That

is the proud owner of one share of school spirit and tradition, manifested in the form of a Bengal Tiger—the Official Mascot of Rochester Institute of Technology.

ROCHESTER INSTITUTE OF TECHNOLOGY "TIGER COMMITTEE"

Printed by Gamma Epsilon Tau, Honorary Graphic Arts Fraternity

Top left: Sign on the Henrietta campus promoting the purchase of a live tiger mascot through "Tiger Stocks," prior to the arrival of Spirit, 1963. *Collection on Spirit (Tiger), RITArc.0035, Box 1, RIT Archives.*

Above: "Tiger Stocks" share certificate, sold for $1 to support Spirit the tiger, 1963. *Collection on Spirit (Tiger), RITArc.0035, Box 1, RIT Archives.*

Top right: "RIT's Flying Tiger Arrives!"—newspaper clipping announcing Spirit's arrival in Rochester, 1963. *Collection on Spirit (Tiger), RITArc.0035, Box 1, RIT Archives.*

Right and bottom right: The RIT Tiger Committee greets Spirit the cub at the Rochester airport, 1963. *Collection on Spirit (Tiger), RITArc.0035, Box 1, RIT Archives.*

BENGAL TIGER MASCOT—Pierre Fontaine, director of the Dallas, Tex., Zoo holds Scheherazade, a 3-months-old Bengal Tiger cub prior to shipment to Rochester, N.Y. The cub was purchased by students of Rochester Institute of Technology as a mascot. (UPI Telephoto.)

RIT Gets a Tiger

It isn't a man-eating hunk of ferocity —yet—but this 2-month-old Bengal tiger is still treated gingerly by Rochester Institute of Technology students today at the Seneca Park Zoo.

The tiger belongs to RIT. It arrived early today from New York City and cost RIT students $1,000, a loan from the student council.

The tiger is representative of RIT athletic teams, and the name, "RIT Tigers," is getting a big push this year.

Students from left are Roger Kramer of New York, James Black, 660 Edgemere Drive, and Dennis Kitchen of Kenmore.

Top left and top right: The RIT Tiger Committee greets Spirit at the airport, featuring David Page in the tiger suit, 1963. *Collection on Spirit (Tiger), RITArc.0035, Box 1, RIT Archives.*

Bottom left: Prior to his flight to Rochester, Spirit is held by Pierre Fontaine at the Dallas Zoo, 1963. *Collection on Spirit (Tiger), RITArc.0035, Box 1, RIT Archives.*

Bottom right: Newspaper article with photos of the RIT Tiger Committee welcoming Spirit the cub at the airport, 1963. *Collection on Spirit (Tiger), RITArc.0035, Box 1, RIT Archives.*

...campus...

Characteristic of man's peculiarities is his use of symbology. On the quad is a large gaily painted rectangular piece of cloth bearing stars and stripes. In physical magnitude not much but within the viewer is the connotation of an expanse of people and territory called the United States. This symbol has been around for some time. But what about tigers? What can we do to associate a meaning between RIT and a Bengal tiger? We have to accept it, then educate the public!

Above: An image from the 1964 *Techmila* showing Spirit the tiger exiting a dance party in RIT's downtown campus dorms. *1964* Techmila, *p. 40, RIT Archives.*

Left: Group portrait of the RIT cheerleaders with Spirit the tiger, the RIT mascot, downtown campus, 1963. *Collection on Spirit (Tiger), RITArc.0035, RIT Archives.*

Throughout the remainder of the 1960s, students increasingly rallied around the tiger mascot as a symbol of their emerging university identity. In the 1964 *Techmila*, students openly reflected on the significance of adopting such a symbol: "Characteristic of man's peculiarities is his use of symbology. On the quad is a large gaily printed rectangular piece of cloth bearing stars and stripes. In physical magnitude not much but within the viewer is the connotation of an expanse of people and territory called the United States. This symbol has been around for some time, but what about tigers? What can we do to associate meaning between RIT and a Bengal Tiger, we have to accept it, then educate the public!"[37]

By invoking the American flag, an icon instantly understood and emotionally charged, the yearbook writers emphasized the work required for the tiger to gain similar symbolic power. Spirit's introduction as a live mascot was a deliberate attempt to establish such meaning in the public imagination. In this, the effort succeeded: Spirit quickly gained popularity at campus events while he was still small enough to make appearances. After Spirit grew too large to attend functions, David Page assumed the role of mascot by donning a tiger costume. The position rapidly became a centerpiece of student life. At athletic events, the mascot energized crowds and became a focal point for school pride. One of Page's fraternity brothers humorously recalled him as "a longitudinally challenged man," which made him the only member who could fit into the hot, uncomfortable suit—but the effort was worth it, as Page was said to be "always surrounded by beautiful women."

The tiger's presence, often alongside cheerleaders, strengthened its ties to athletics and student celebrations, while also remaining closely connected to fraternity culture.[38] One of Spirit's earliest introductions occurred at a Wednesday night fraternity and sorority gathering on Troup Street, then home to many Greek organizations. Jim Black, a member of the original Tiger Committee, recalled: "Very shortly after that, he made his first appearance at a basketball game at the gym. And it was the largest crowd we ever had. The students really jumped on the idea that we had our very own frosh-eating tiger." Black added that at a time when there were concerns about student apathy, fellow student Denis wrote to the editor describing the mascot as "the best thing to end student apathy," a sentiment Black fully endorsed. The tiger had done what it was intended to do: it became a unifying force, a source of excitement, and a living emblem of campus pride.

While students organized the fundraising and purchase of the tiger, campus administrators played an essential role in ensuring its safe arrival and presence. They assisted with logistics, including securing insurance to allow the mascot to be legally and safely associated with the institute. One such administrator was Steve Miller, the director of student activities, who, according to those involved, "came to RIT at a time when the institute needed somebody who was really going to pull things together from the student point of view."[39] Committee member Francis Millor reflected on Miller's impact: "He did some really great things. He put together a number of different programs so there was a lot more activity on campus." Miller proved instrumental in shaping the student culture that would come to define RIT, orchestrating Spirit's arrival—including arranging for American Airlines to transport the cub free of charge—and supporting fraternity and sorority programming in which Alpha Pi Omega members were deeply involved.

The Tiger Committee also credited Dr. Mark Ellingson, RIT's president at the time, as another key supporter. Dr. Ellingson had hired Steve Miller to lead student activities

Left: An image showcasing a full spread of Spirit the tiger in the 1964 *Techmila*. *1964* Techmila, *p. 201, RIT Archives.*

Right: A full-page image of Spirit the tiger in his enclosure at the zoo, at the end of the 1963 *Techmila*. *1963* Techmila, *RIT Archives.*

and had endorsed the tiger initiative. Known for his role in relocating the campus from downtown Rochester to Henrietta, Ellingson had a notable presence among students. Roger Kramer described him as "formidable," a stern figure who nevertheless could "walk around campus and greet everyone by name." He continued: "He was the man who had the vision that RIT was on the cusp of becoming something so much greater. He's the man who ultimately lit all the fuses."

Dr. Ellingson personally attended Spirit's arrival at the airport, standing alongside David Page as they welcomed the new mascot. For him, the tiger was not merely symbolic—it was a strategic publicity opportunity to showcase RIT's evolution. As Jim Black explained in an interview with Kramer: "He realized the tiger was publicity. I'm sure there's still news coverage of the tiger arriving, and there's television programs, and he was covered when he came to the basketball games, when he went to the hockey games, when he went to different schools. It was great publicity for the school. Great publicity. And basically free."

For both the administration and the president, Spirit became a powerful representation of institutional transformation. The mascot helped define RIT's identity as it entered a new era—not just as an accredited academic institution, but as a university with a vibrant and recognizable student culture.

Mascots in American higher education date back to at least the 1880s, when a Princeton newspaper first referred to its athletes as "the Tigers." From there, naming sports teams after symbols of strength and competitive spirit became a widespread trend. Drawing inspiration from medieval heraldry—with its crests, colors, and emblems—college students across the country began adopting mascots and school colors to express group identity. The rise of Greek life and organized athletics, both highly visible and socially influential forces on campus, fueled demands for unifying symbols that could represent the student body as a whole.

Mascots served multiple functions: they were believed to bring luck, they energized fans, and they embodied institutional values and norms. Schools selected mascots based on a variety of influences, including mythology and folklore, local geography, and traditional regional symbols. In some cases, religion, ethnicity,

Above: President Mark Ellingson welcomes the tiger mascot, 1963.
RIT Institutional Photograph collection, RITArc.0762, Box 509, RIT Archives.
Top right: A photo of David Page in his Tiger Mascot costume posing with the RIT cheerleaders in 1964. *1964* Techmila, *pg. 191, RIT Archives.*
Bottom right: David Page and a sorority member show off tiger mascot suits; Page's APO fraternity symbol is visible on his arm. *Collection on Spirit (Tiger), RITArc.0035, Box 1, RIT Archives.*

HOCKEY

Organized as a varsity sport in 1965, hockey passed this year, as in their past season, practice does pay off well. At season's end, the icers had a Finger Lakes League record of 14-7-1, and clinched third place in the annual FLHL Tournament in March 1969.

Coach Darryl Sullivan can be credited for turning out one of the strongest and fastest teams in the state, in spite of losses to tough Oswego, Hamilton, and University of Buffalo squads, the Tigers showed remarkable tenacity when skating against the stronger teams, often loosing only by a few goals. As one spectator remarked at a home game this year, "they never give up. If the other team makes just one mistake, the Tigers are halfway down the ice before the other team even realizes what's happening."

Much of the credit can be given to three outstanding players—Dennis Lepley, Ken Vokac and Mark Dougherty. Lepley scored 29 goals during the season in the center position; Vokac worked the defense positions, making some 18 goals and 24 assists in 24 games played. Goalie Mark Dougherty averaged some 40 saves a game, and is generally acknowledged to be the best goalie in Tiger history. All three were elected to the Finger Lakes All-League team for their fine individual performances.

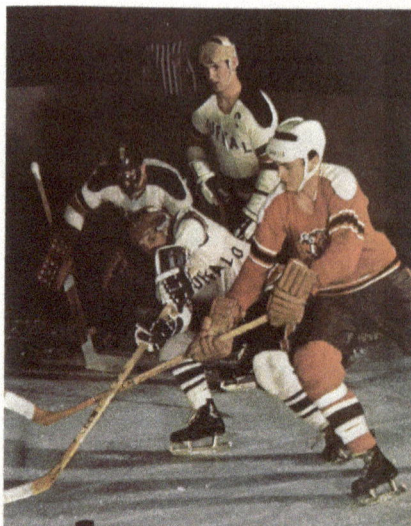

Top left and right: RIT hockey uniforms feature the "roaring tiger" logo for the first time, 1969. *1969 Techmila, pp. 242–44. RIT Archives.*

Above: RIT women's fencing team wearing merchandise with an early tiger logo in blue and gray. *1963 Techmila, p. 193. RIT Archives.*

Above right: The aforementioned tiger logo on merchandise with blue and grey coloring, as seen on a women's fencing hoodie, 1960s. *RIT Graphic Identification System collection, RITArc.0201, RIT Merchandising, RIT Archives.*

Right: The official "RIT Tigers Bar," sold briefly in the campus store during the 1960s. *Collection on Spirit (Tiger), RITArc.0035, Box 1, Folder 3, RIT Archives.*

or national identity played central roles in shaping mascot choices.[40]

Beyond cultural meaning, mascots quickly became powerful marketing tools. As branding became increasingly intertwined with institutional identity, mascots provided a memorable and emotionally resonant way for colleges to define themselves. They offered a sense of belonging and communal connection, "a means by which we as individuals can find common ground, integrate with one another, and find personal meaning within large groups."[41] At RIT, Spirit the tiger and the Tiger symbol fulfilled exactly this role. Even after the live mascot passed away, its symbolic legacy remained deeply rooted in campus life—visible in the architecture of the new Henrietta campus and in the collective identity of students, faculty, staff, and alumni. The tiger appeared everywhere: on uniforms, flags, promotional materials, and even custom-made candy bars. What began as a designation for athletes soon expanded to represent the entire university community.

RIT's hockey team was among the first to wear a roaring tiger design, debuting in 1969. Shortly thereafter, the word "Tigers" appeared on their jerseys, signaling a broader institutional embrace of the mascot. The tiger also shaped the development of official school colors during the relocation and concurrent rebranding process. As part of this shift, RIT adopted two Pantone colors: orange and brown.

According to the 2005 *RIT Identity Manual*, "This concept was tied loosely to the colors of the tiger, and an analysis of what colors were already in use by other universities."[42] The manual further notes that "the colors were refined to burnt umber and orange to correspond more closely to the brickwork of the new campus." This rebranding marked a significant departure from earlier years, when the Rochester Athenaeum and Mechanics Institute identified with blue and gray.

As part of RIT's new visual identity, two tiger emblems were developed: the walking tiger and the roaring tiger. These mascot graphics were primarily reserved for athletics, alumni relations, and student activities, and they were governed by strict usage rules; for example, they were never to be printed at an angle. While the tiger served as the vibrant and energetic symbol of student culture, the university also introduced two additional seals to reflect its institutional legacy and architectural aesthetic. The Official Institute Seal and the Contemporary Seal referenced RIT's origins as the Mechanics Institute and echoed the functional, Brutalist design of the new Henrietta campus, establishing a broader identity beyond the mascot alone.[43]

RIT's identity came to be expressed through multiple visual elements, each representing different facets of university life. The seals embodied the institution's formal character, history, and academic values, while the tiger represented the lived experience of students and the spirit of community life. As the 1963 *Techmila* observed, "An institution's symbol reflects its outward character and inner guiding philosophy, its approach to the society of which it is a part; change and flux in an institution are represented in the transition of its emblem." The campus relocation demanded a comprehensive rebranding, and the resulting visual identity served as "evidence of the changing and dynamic growth of RIT."

This updated design system sought to align with the ideals of progress, modernity, and permanence embodied in the architecture of the new Henrietta campus, envisioned as RIT's long-term home. A later identity manual explained: "RIT's graphic mark was designed at the time RIT moved to the new campus and is symbolic of the environmental quality of space and architecture of the new facilities. This revised graphic identity mark, an evolution of a previous mark, was developed to exist as a single strong, unchanging image."

Top left: RIT flag, ca. 1970. *RIT Graphic Identification System collection, RITArc.0201, RIT Archives.*

Top right: As the university was rebranding, inital design options included using the RIT title, with the original Mechanics Institute colors of blue and gray. *RIT Graphic Identification System collection, RIT.0201, RIT Archives.*

Right above: RIT logo mockup, ca. 1970. *RIT Graphic Identification System collection, RITArc.0201, RIT Archives.*

Right center: RIT seals, ca. 1970. *RIT Graphic Identification System collection, RITArc.0201, RIT Archives.*

Right below: RIT logo mockup, ca. 1970. *RIT Graphic Identification System collection, RITArc.0201, RIT Archives.*

Far right: RIT seals, ca. 1970. *RIT Graphic Identification System collection, RITArc.0201, RIT Archives.*

Logotype designs and sketches by Bob Wright, 1962. *RIT Graphic Identification System collection, RITArc.0201, RIT Archives.*

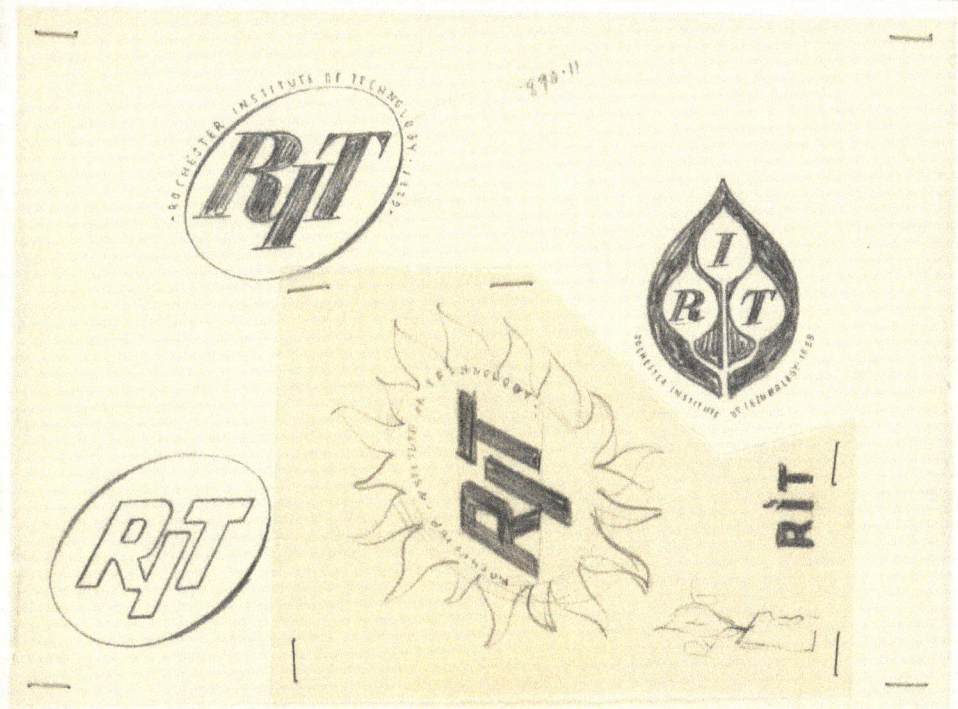

Above: Eric Senna (left) and Fred Smith (right) at the tiger sculpture unveiling and dedication ceremony, 1989. *Eric Senna papers, RITArc.0812, RIT Archives.*

Right: Fred Smith speaking at the tiger sculpture unveiling and dedication ceremony, 1989. *Eric Senna papers, RITArc.0812, RIT Archives.*

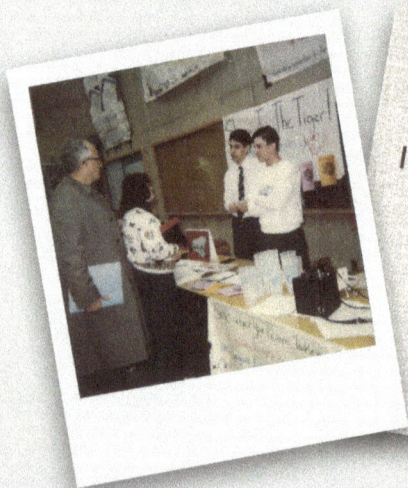

I BROKE GROUND AT R.I.T.

*Campus Life Center
Parents' Weekend
October 21, 1989*

Far left: Students tabling to advertise the groundbreaking event, 1989. *Eric Senna papers, RITArc.0812, RIT Archives.*

Left: Takeaway from the groundbreaking event, 1989. *Eric Senna papers, RITArc.0812, RIT Archives.*

Reshaping Campus:
"In Pursuit of Tradition, Spirit, and Pride"

The first Tiger Committee of the 1960s did more than bring a live tiger to campus; it helped lay the foundation for a new kind of student culture at RIT. Spirit quickly became a rallying point, a symbol of pride that offered students a sense of shared identity the institute had previously lacked. The tiger mascot not only energized student life but also became deeply integrated into institutional identity, eventually influencing the school's official colors and branding. This era paved the way for a cultural shift that continued into the 1970s, coinciding with the move to the new Henrietta campus. Removed from the urban environment of downtown Rochester, the suburban campus fostered the development of a more cohesive, community-oriented student experience, one centered on belonging and school spirit.

While much of this transformation was initiated by students, the administration also recognized the need to support and formalize student life. To bridge growing tensions between students and faculty—exacerbated by the political atmosphere of the 1960s—RIT established a new leadership role: Vice President of Student Affairs. The position was filled by Dr. Fred W. Smith, a professor from Michigan State University, who was charged with strengthening faculty-student relationships, revising curriculum to ease academic strain, and cultivating a more engaging social environment.

With the transition to the new campus, cracks in student satisfaction became more visible. Many students felt that the institution remained overly rigid and academically intense without providing sufficient outlets for recreation and community-building. Dr. Smith sought to address this disconnect by proposing initiatives such as a student recreational center that would serve as a gathering space for fostering campus spirit and social cohesion.

At its core, RIT had long been a career-oriented institution, valued for its technical rigor and practical education. Yet, as Dr. Smith noted, this strength came with a cost. In his assessment of campus life, he wrote: "Students comment on the lack of social life, campus traditions, school spirit, pride, and sense of community. They feel RIT lacks student life facilities that equal those available in the academic areas."[44] Spirit the tiger may have served as the spark for a new identity, but Smith's vision aimed to build the broader infrastructure needed to sustain a true sense of university community. Together, student-led initiatives and administrative support created momentum for a richer, more unified campus culture, one that extended far beyond the mascot itself.

One of RIT's mission statements was "to prepare graduates with such knowledge and background as will enable them to enrich themselves intellectually, culturally, physically, and spiritually." President M. Richard Rose and the RIT Board of Trustees supported a proposal centered on establishing a comprehensive campus-life complex that would include a Student Center, a Counseling Center, and the NTID Department of Psychological Services—grouped under student health services. This project was intended to strengthen morale and support the educational mission by improving student health, enhancing recruitment and retention, boosting academic performance, increasing engagement between deaf and hearing students, and fostering overall pride and community spirit.

The initiatives known as a "complementary education program" were aimed at "educating the whole person." It represented a philosophical shift in how RIT approached learning, aligning with the evolving understandings of mental, physical, and emotional wellness emerging in the 1970s. The goal was to cultivate not just technical

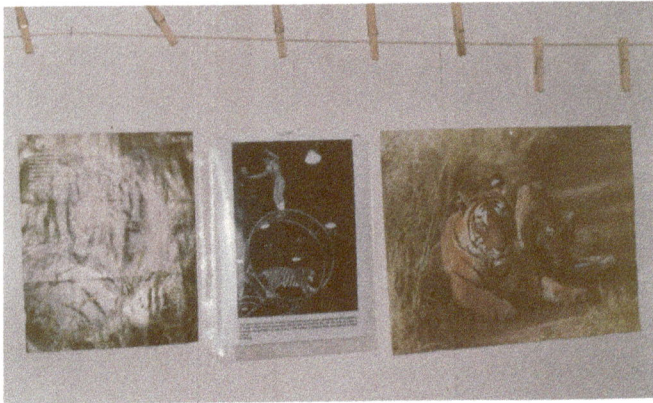

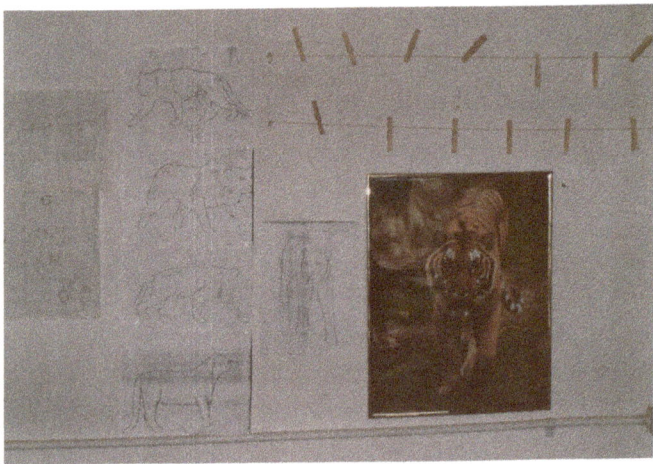

Research and sketches in the design process of building the tiger statue. *Eric Senna papers, RITArc.0812, RIT Archives.*

competence, but also social and interpersonal development through intentional relationship-building, community activities, and cocurricular engagement. Student organizations, including Student Government, rallied behind these ideas—not because RIT lacked academic prestige, but because student expectations were changing.

In his proposal for a modern student life center, Smith argued that such investments were critical to remaining competitive: "RIT is well known and highly regarded academically, including its laboratories, workshops, and studios. It does lack, in the perception of many prospective students, in the extra-academic diversity and opportunities that are in evidence at our competitor institutions."[45] As student enrollment continued to rise and athletics and campus clubs grew in popularity, the university recognized the need for infrastructure that supported student life beyond the classroom.

In a paper presented at a 1973 National Association of Student Personnel Administrators (NASPA) conference, Smith cited *The Chronicle of Higher Education* to reflect changing student expectations: "The student wants desperately to be engaged in his education; he is tired of 'going through college' without knowing what he went through. I predict, therefore, that we will return before long to the idea of this 'whole student' whose life style and philosophical basis may be just as important to us as the completion of curriculum requirements used to be." Smith's role and initiatives were deeply rooted in this belief: that student life and academic life were interdependent, and that a thriving student body required both community and identity.

In 1989, the student-initiated project to create a life-size bronze tiger statue became perhaps the greatest legacy of student leadership at RIT. Proposed by student Eric Senna, the vice chairman of the student directorate and the chair of the second Tiger Committee, the statue was envisioned as a symbol to continue RIT's cultural tradition and to keep the memory of Spirit alive.

In his 1989 proposal for the statue's placement, Senna wrote: "RIT has worked hard to develop school spirit and an atmosphere of tradition and pride on its campus. . . . The RIT Tiger sculpture is a perfect example of such an opportunity."[46] Senna noted that many students lamented the lack of a central spot for graduation photos or a defining landmark that communicated school identity. The stark brick architecture of the Henrietta campus embodied institutional ideals, but students longed for a symbolic focal point—something akin to mascot statues found at peer institutions.

Mirroring the original Spirit fundraising campaign, the committee issued "stocks" for $3 each, featuring an image of the roaring tiger face, along with signatures from the university president, the sculptor, and Senna, labeled the "Initiator." Each share bore the phrase "In Pursuit of Tradition, Spirit, and Pride" in gold tiger print, and contributors who purchased ten or more would have their names commemorated on a plaque.

Student Government voted to allocate $8,000 from the student directory fund, with the remaining $50,000 for the statue, pedestal, and landscaping to be raised through donations, stock sales, and university support. Not all students initially supported the idea. In a faxed message, one student named Jeffrey questioned the statue's relevance: "Why are we getting it. Please do not tell me that Penn State has one so we should have one. I believe RIT has its own identity and doesn't need to borrow from other campuses. I do not understand why everyone is hoping that RIT students will take their grad pictures in front of it. Why do they want to start a tradition that isn't even original. Usually traditions 'just happen' and [are] not planned by the few."[47]

Committee members—including Senna, financial coordinator Daniel Greenberg, and Stephen L. Schultz

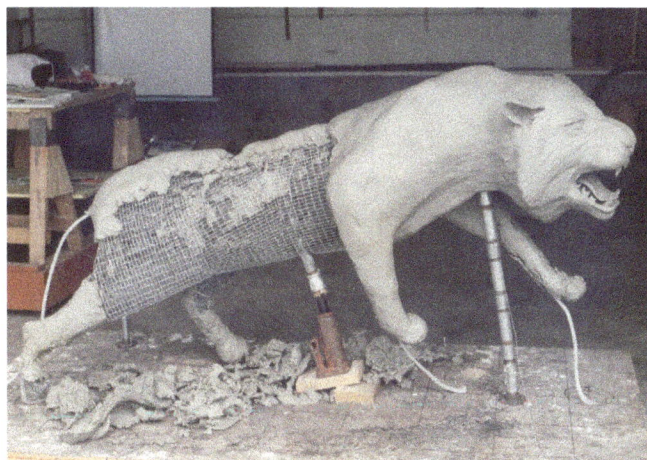

Tiger statue in process, 1989. *Eric Senna papers, RITArc.0812, RIT Archives.*

29

(the student directorate director of Student Relations)—
responded in detail. Greenberg addressed questions of
identity most directly, countering: "Do you really think
RIT has an identity? I think we're trying to create one. A
sense of pride and tradition that RIT doesn't seem to have
much of!" Schultz tackled concerns about traditions by
pointing out: "As far as traditions 'just happening,' they
have to start somewhere. It is not as if this is going to be a
'mandated tradition' at RIT, but this statue does provide a
place where traditions may get started."

Concerns over funding were also resolved: excess
funds would be placed in an endowment for scholarships
and grants for students whose involvement in clubs and
campus leadership reduced their working hours.[48] In this
way, the tiger statue would not only stand as a physical
symbol of campus pride but also materially support
future student leaders.

The committee also gave careful thought to selecting
a sculptor. After consulting with an RIT professor, they
identified local artist D. H. S. (Duff) Wehle, known for
his background in zoology and environmental sciences
and his desire to express "the inter-relationships among
animals and between animals and their environment"
through sculpture.[49] Senna and Wehle discussed pose,
scale, and placement, ultimately deciding on a life-size
roaring tiger, approximately 4 feet tall and 10 feet long,
evoking the official RIT mascot. The final sculpture,
mounted on a rock base, weighed roughly 2 tons and cost
an estimated $50,000.

From the first committee meeting on April 26, 1989,
to the statue's unveiling on November 10 of that same
year, the project took just over six months, a powerful testament to the continued student drive to shape
RIT's culture.

Above: Tiger statue in process, 1989. *Eric Senna papers, RITArc.0812, RIT Archives.*

Right: Eric Senna, D. H. S. "Duff" Wehle, Fred Smith, President Rose, and John Simmons standing around the newly installed tiger statue, 1989. *Eric Senna papers, RITArc.0812, RIT Archives.*

Ritchie, the RIT mascot,
parachutes into a soccer
game from a helicopter,
1987. Gelatin silver print.
RIT Institutional Photography
collection, RITArc.0762,
Box 575, RIT Archives.

Today, the RIT Tiger statue stands outside the Student Hall for Exploration and Development (SHED), having been relocated during the building's construction. This is the statue's third home—it was first moved from its original placement near the Campus Connections bookstore to the grassy quad space outside Midnight Oil Coffee Shop, before being restored to a central location where it now anchors student life between the Wallace Library and the Student Union.

At its dedication in 1989, Eric Senna expressed his hopes for the statue's impact: "The tiger stands as a potential link or bond between the institute as a whole and the students of RIT. Our hope is that it will build Institute-wide spirit and pride."[50] President Rose, Vice President of Student Affairs Dr. Fred Smith, and sculptor Duff Wehle joined Senna at the unveiling, emphasizing student leadership as being central to RIT's evolving identity. After twenty-one years on the Henrietta campus, the statue symbolized not only a new era but also the longevity of student-driven tradition.

The story of RIT's student culture is one of initiative, voice, and continuity. From the early publications of *PSIMAR* and the *Ramikin*, which gave students a platform to define their identity, to the *Reporter*, which continues that legacy today, student-led media shaped perspectives and preserved campus memory. Greek life also remained a cornerstone. Today, twenty-nine international and national fraternities and sororities—including thirteen multicultural organizations governed by the Multicultural Greek Council (MGC)—promote leadership, service, and community. Signature campus traditions, such as Mud Tug—an annual charity tug-of-war hosted by Zeta Tau Alpha and Phi Kappa Psi—continue to raise thousands of dollars for local causes, with the 2024 event generating over $10,000 for the Hillside Family of Agencies.[51]

Athletics, another foundational element of Tiger spirit, has expanded significantly. RIT now fields twenty-four varsity teams, including two NCAA Division I hockey programs and multiple Division III teams, involving more than 675 student-athletes. Recent campus developments, including the Gene Polisseni Center (2014) and the soon-to-be-completed Tiger Stadium (2026), further reinforce athletics as a pillar of student engagement. Beneath varsity-level competition thrives a robust ecosystem of club and intramural sports, supported by facilities in the Hale-Andrews Student Life Center—an institution aligned with Dr. Smith's legacy of holistic student development. Ritchie the Tiger, the costumed mascot, remains a beloved figure at games and events, continuing the tradition David Page once embodied in the 1960s.

In 1989, the same year the statue was installed, the Tiger Committee hosted a naming contest for the mascot. Options ranged from "Tony" ("It's grrrreat!") to "Big Ben." The winning name, submitted by student Richard Mislan, was "Ritchie." Mislan won a $50 campus store certificate, which he used to purchase a hockey jersey, and Ritchie has been the mascot's name ever since. Now central to campus traditions, Ritchie appears at Brick City Homecoming, FreezeFest, Imagine RIT, and Orientation, including the release of the iconic "Ritchie Balloons." Mislan later authored *Ritchie Finds His Stripes*, a children's book inspired by sculptor Duff Wehle's challenge to "breathe life" into the mascot, as well as by Mislan's daughters.[52]

Ultimately, RIT's campus culture has been shaped—again and again—by student creativity, collaboration, and persistence. What began as a joke in a 1950s April Fools article became a legacy of spirit, tradition, and pride that continues to evolve with each generation. From conventions like Tora-Con ("Tora" meaning tiger in

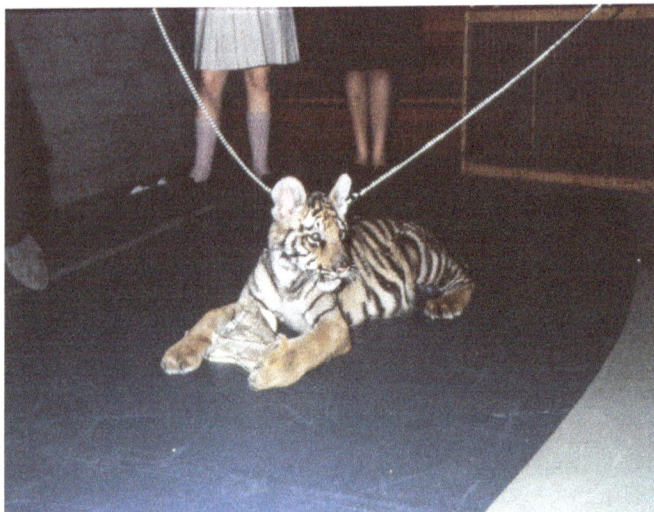

Spirit, the live Bengal tiger cub mascot, holds a sneaker while handled on two leashes, 1963. *Fred Smith papers, RITArc.0074, RIT Archives.*

Spirit the tiger visits the library with an unknown student, 1963. *RIT Institutional Photography collection, RITArc.0762, Box 509, RIT Archives.*

Japanese, originally considered as a name for the Bengal cub) to graduation photos with champagne beside the statue, sweaters wrapped around its neck in winter, and Polaroids taken with Ritchie on Accepted Students' Day, student life revolves around Tiger symbolism as a marker of belonging.

Nearly two centuries since its founding, RIT continues to grow in size, innovation, and tradition. As it approaches its bicentennial in 2029, new customs will no doubt emerge, but the unifying force of Tiger spirit endures. The statue remains a central landmark, and the mascot lives on through hoodies, jerseys, stickers, sculptures, and shared memories, embodying what it means to be part of the Rochester Institute of Technology.

A portrait of Spirit, the RIT tiger mascot, as the RIT *Reporter* cover in color, 1963.

Notes

1   Helen Lefkowitz Horowitz, *Campus Life: Undergraduate Cultures from the End of the Eighteenth Century to the Present* (University of Chicago Press, 1988).

2   Dane R. Gordon, *Rochester Institute of Technology: Industrial Development and Educational Innovation in an American City, 1829–2006* (RIT Press, 2007).

3   Eugene C. Colby, scrapbook, unidentified paper, "Our Industrial Interests," RIT Archives, 2.

4   Gordon, *Rochester Institute of Technology*, 30.

5   "Morrill Act (1862)," National Archives and Records Administration, accessed June 20, 2025, https://www.archives.gov/milestone-documents/morrill-act.

6   Horowitz, *Campus Life*, 5.

7   Gordon, *Rochester Institute of Technology,* 51.

8   Horowitz, *Campus Life*.

9   Horowitz, *Campus Life*, 42.

10   The students of Rochester Athenaeum and Mechanics Institute, *The M.I. Book, Volume One* (Rochester Press, 1912).

11   Gordon, *Rochester Institute of Technology*, 115.

12   Gordon, *Rochester Institute of Technology*, 121–22.

13   RAMI students, *M.I. Book, Volume One*, 111.

14   Horowitz, *Campus Life*, 193.

15   Ortiz-Martínez, Gabriela, Patricia Vázquez-Villegas, María Ileana Ruiz-Cantisani, Mónica Delgado-Fabián, Danna A Conejo-Márquez, and Jorge Membrillo-Hernández, "Analysis of the Retention of Women in Higher Education Stem Programs," humanities and social sciences communications, 2023, https://pmc.ncbi.nlm.nih.gov/articles/PMC10007666/#CR70.

16   The students of Rochester Athenaeum and Mechanics Institute, *The M.I. Book, Volume Eighteen* (Rochester Press, 1929), 127–28.

17   RAMI Students, *M.I. Book, Volume Eighteen*, 81.

18   The students of Rochester Athenaeum and Mechanics Institute, *The PSIMAR, Volume 1. Number 2* (Rochester Press, November 16, 1928), 5.

19   Gordon, *Rochester Institute of Technology*, 206.

20   Labaree, David F. "Learning to Love the Bomb: The Cold War Brings the Best Of . . . ," January 2016, https://dlabaree.people.stanford.edu/sites/g/files/sbiybj25186/files/media/file/learning_to_love_the_bomb_-_published_version_1.pdf.

21   Labaree, "Learning to Love the Bomb."

22   "Servicemen's Readjustment Act (1944)," National Archives and Records Administration, accessed June 26, 2025, https://www.archives.gov/milestone-documents/servicemens-readjustment-act.

23   Gregory McNamee, *The GI Bill: Evolving Benefits*, the VVA veteran, a publication of Vietnam Veterans of America, January 2020, https://vvaveteran.org/40-1/40-1_gibill.html.

24   The numbers were approximately 21 percent white soldiers dishonorably discharged to 39 percent Black soldiers.

25   George T. Mazuzan, "The National Science Foundation: A Brief History," *National Science Foundation*, accessed June 26, 2025, https://www.nsf.gov/about/history/narrative.

26   "Sputnik Spurs Passage of the National Defense Education Act," US Senate: Sputnik Spurs Passage of the National Defense Education Act, September 8, 2023, https://www.senate.gov/artandhistory/history/minute/Sputnik_Spurs_Passage_of_National_Defense_Education_Act.htm.

27   Gordon, *Rochester Institute of Technology,* 232.

28   Gordon, *Rochester Institute of Technology,* 232.

29   Gordon, *Rochester Institute of Technology,* 249.

30   Georgia Pressley and Terrell Brooks, "Then vs. Now: How the Story of Rochester's Inner Loop Has Changed," *Democrat and Chronicle*, November 7, 2023, https://www.democratandchronicle.com/story/news/2023/11/07/rochester-inner-loop-history-coverage-in-the-democrat-and-chronicle/70533488007/.

31   RIT *Reporter* Staff, "*Reporter* — May 19th 1961" (1961), accessed from https://repository.rit.edu/unipubs/1483.

32 Gordon, *Rochester Institute of Technology,*277.

33 Scott Bureau, "Celebrating 50 Years at the Henrietta Campus," RIT News, August 6, 2018, https://www.rit.edu/news/celebrating-50-years-henrietta-campus-0.

34 RIT *Techmila* Staff, *Techmila 1964* (1964).

35 RIT *Reporter* Staff, "RIT *Reporter* — March 12th 1956" (1956), accessed from https://repository.rit.edu/unipubs/1585.

36 RIT *Reporter* Staff, "RIT *Reporter* — March 29th 1957" (1957), accessed from https://repository.rit.edu/unipubs/1570

37 RIT *Techmila* Staff, *Techmila 1964* (1964).

38 At Brigham Young University (BYU), their live mascot, a cougar, was also managed by the Alpha Phi Omega chapter, the same fraternity that formed the Tiger Committee at RIT.

39 Oral History Tiger Reunion Interview with David Page '66 (Photo Science), Jim Black '64 (Chemistry), Denis Kitchen '65 (Printing), Roger Kramer '65 (Photo Science), Francis "Skip" Millor '65 (Photo Science), 2005-10-07." Interview by Becky Simmons, Kathy Lindsley, and Judy Sidlauskas, October 7, 2005. Collection on Spirit (Tiger) (RITArc.0035).

40 Garry Gennar DeSantis, "Collegiate Symbols and Mascots of the American Landscape: Identity, Iconography, and Marketing," FSU Digital Repository, 2018, https://repository.lib.fsu.edu/islandora/object/fsu:661130/datastream/PDF/view.

41 Stanley Ryan Viner, "Branding a University's Mascot," eGrove, 2011, https://egrove.olemiss.edu/hon_thesis/2143/.

42 RIT Identity Manual general history, ca-2005/2006, RIT Graphic Identification System Collection, Box #1, Folder "Publications," RIT Archives, Rochester Institute of Technology.

43 "Graphic Mark: one man's cup of tea . . . another's poison" via the RIT Graphic Identification System Collections RITArc.0201, Box One, Folder "Publications," RIT Archives, Rochester Institute of Technology.

44 "Proposed Student Life Complex Rationale & Description," F. Smith, RIT Archives, RITArc.0074, Fred Smith Papers, 1975–1984.

45 "Student Life Complex," F. Smith, RIT Archives, RITArc.0074, Fred Smith Papers, 1975–1984.

46 "Proposal From Rochester Institute of Technology for Site Development and Endowment for the RIT Tiger," Eric Senna, RIT Archives, Eric Senna Papers, RITArc.0812 Box #1, Folder 7, 1989.

47 "ACC_User:[Notes$Library]College_Life.Note;5 — College Life — " Eric Senna, RIT Archives, Eric Senna Papers, RITArc.0812 Box #1, Folder 6 "Tiger Statue background and questions, printed RIT VAX messages, 1989."

48 "ACC_User:[Notes$Library]College_Life.Note;5 — College Life — " Eric Senna, RIT Archives, Eric Senna Papers, RITArc.0812 Box #1, Folder 6 "Tiger Statue background and questions, printed RIT VAX messages, 1989.

49 "Communication with Eric Senna," D. H. S Wehle, RIT Archives, Eric Senna Papers, RITArc.0812 Box #1, Folder 2 "Duff Wehle correspondence, notes, sketches, and references, 1989."

50 *RIT News & Events* 21, no. 8, November 16, 1989, RIT News & Events staff, RIT Archives, Eric Senna Papers, RITArc.0812 Box #1, Folder 15 "RIT Bengal Tiger Copyright and Registration Statue, 1990."

51 A joint Instagram post between RIT Mud Tug and Hillside Family of Agencies shared a picture of the teams posing with a check showing the total amount: "We are grateful to @phisirit and @zta_rit for raising an amazing $10,350 at their annual @ritmudtug. For 14 years, they've hosted this fundraising event in support of our mission. Thank you for your continuous generosity!"

52 Rick Mislan, "Ritchie Finds His Stripes," accessed August 14, 2025, https://www.ritchiefindshisstripes.com/RITchie.php.

Acknowledgments

RIT Archives Staff and Student Employees

Elizabeth Call, University Archivist
Landyn Hatch, Innovation and Engagement
Archivist
Jennifer Roeszies, Archives Assistant
Claire Gallucci (Museum Studies, Anthropology,
and Art History)
Renee Guerin (Museum Studies and Fine Arts)
Lydia Hammer, copyeditor extraordinaire
(Journalism and English)

Additional Support

Fred Smith, former vice president for Student
Affairs (1971–1993) and secretary of the institute and
assistant to the president (1993–2008); major thanks
to Fred for his support.
Eric Senna (BS '91), member of RIT's Alumni
Association Board and former vice president of the
student directorate; his collection in Archives, Eric
Senna papers (RITArc.0812), proved invaluable to
the author's research.

Reviewers

Patrick Williams, Humanities Librarian, Lead
Librarian for Digital and Open Scholarship, Syracuse
University Libraries
Marilyn Parrish, Consultant

About the Author

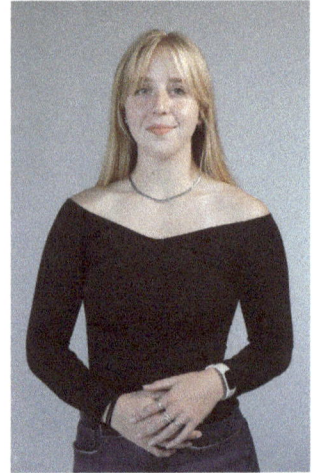

Autumn Bernava is a third-year student at Rochester Institute of Technology, pursuing a BFA in photojournalism. She works for the RIT Athletic Communications department, as well as the RIT Archives. She is also a member of the Women's Track and Field team and RIT NPPA.

Outside of sports, Bernava enjoys working with the local community, especially regarding family-run agriculture, literary spaces, and animal rescues. Currently based out of Rochester, New York, she grew up in Columbus, Ohio, often spending time with her mother on her farm.

When not working or attending track practice, Bernava can often be found hiking or at home reading with her cat, Midge.